The Mother on Japan

Impressum

Acknowledgments: I had everything to learn in Japan. For four years, from an artistic point of view, I lived from wonder to wonder . . . And everything in this city, in this country, from beginning to end, gives you the impression of impermanence, of the unexpected, the exceptional. You always come to things you did not expect; you want to find them again and they are lost – they have made something else which is equally charming. From the artistic point of view, the point of view of beauty, I don't think there is a country as beautiful as that.

First Edition 2010
Second Edition 2022
The Mother on Japan
Prisma

ISBN 978-93-95460-06-4 (print)
ISBN 978-93-95460-07-1 (ebook)

BISAC Code:
TRV003050, TRAVEL / Asia / East / Japan
BIO000000, BIOGRAPHY & AUTOBIOGRAPHY / General
PHI034000, PHILOSOPHY / Social
ART019030 ART / Asian / Japanese

Thema Subject Category:
AB, The arts: general topics
JBCC, Cultural studies

Cataloging-in-Publication Data for this title is available from the Library of Congress.

Printed and bound in India by:
PRISMA, Aurelec/ Prayogshala,
Auroville 605101, Tamil Nadu, India

Digital Editions produced by:
DMI Systems Pvt Ltd, Vishnupuri,
Aligarh 202001, Uttar Pradesh, India

Published by PRISMA, an imprint of Digital Media Initiatives
www.prisma.haus, www.dmi.systems

Contents

Let the eternal Light dawn

on the eastern horizon.

Let the Supreme Beauty be manifest
in this land of beauty so close to my heart.

The Mother's message to Japan, 1962

Japan was in the physical world

the teacher of beauty.

She must not renounce her privilege.

The Mother's message for the Sri Aurobindo Society.
Osaka, Japan, on 16th October 1972.

INTRODUCTION

During the first World War it was not possible for Paul Richard and Mirra Richard to go to India, but it was possible for them to go to Japan. In the First World War Japan was an ally of Great Britain and therefore of Great Britain's allies, including France. Paul Richard received a commission to promote the export of French products to China and Japan.

As the Mother later said, it was not all that difficult to get this kind of overseas commission, for nobody else wanted to run the risk of a sea voyage to Japan.

Many formalities were required in London before they could board, on 11th March 1916, the Kamo Maru – the same Japanese ship that had brought them from Colombo to France a year before. This time the Richards did not travel alone. They were accompanied by an English lady, Miss Dorothy Hodgson, of whom all that is known is that her fiancé had died, that therefore she never wanted to marry, and that she had chosen Mirra as her spiritual mentor. Dorothy Hodgson, later named Datta by Sri Aurobindo, would remain with the Mother for the rest of her life.

Somewhere in the Atlantic Ocean the Kamo Maru was approached threateningly by 'a very big ship', which was most probably a German battleship. The incident happened around four o'clock in the morning and Mirra, an early riser, was the only one among the passengers to observe it. There was an exchange of signals, the warship slowly circled around the Kamo Maru, and then suddenly continued on its course. When Mirra asked the Japanese captain, with whom she had sympathized since the beginning of the journey, and of whom she had drawn a sketch, what had happened, he asked her to

tell nobody what she had seen. For he had signalled the warship that he had a gun on board, and threatened to fire. In actual fact he had no gun, and his bravado had put his passengers and his ship in jeopardy. On 6 April 1916 the Kamo Maru dropped anchor at Table Bay, and the Richards visited Cape Town, the capital of South Africa. More than a month later, on 9 and 10 May, the ship called at Shanghai, where Mirra caught a whiff of China. On 18 May the Kamo Maru docked at Yokohama, the largest Japanese port.

Tokyo

The first year of their stay in Japan was spent for the most part in Tokyo, in the house of Dr Shumei Okawa and his wife. Okawa was a university professor in Tokyo, teaching Asian History. He was also a member of the Black Dragon Society and the leading spirit of the pan-Asiatic movement in Japan… a person of considerable influence, who was deeply interested in Indian affairs and was bitterly opposed to British rule in India. K.R. Srinivasa Iyengar met him in 1957. Okawa had become practically blind and was an invalid, but his mind was still very much alive and his memory clear.

In June 1916 the Richards met Rabindranath Tagore, who had come to Japan on a lecture tour. Mirra made a fine pencil sketch of him on 11 June, the day he delivered a speech at the Imperial University in Tokyo, 'The Message of India to Japan'. Tagore had become world-famous in 1913, when he was awarded the Nobel Prize for his volume of poetry 'Gitanjali'.

The Richards would meet Tagore again in 1919, when they stayed in the same hotel for some time. In 1901 Tagore had founded an educational institute, Shantiniketan (Place of Peace).

Among the other people the Richards met in Tokyo was 'a son of Tolstoy'.

Two months after their arrival, on 7 July, Mirra published an article in Fujoshimbwi, a Japanese paper, entitled 'Woman and the War'. The article starts as follows: "You have asked me what I think of the feminist movement and what will be the consequences of the present war for it. One of the first effects of the war has certainly been to give quite a new aspect to the question. The futility of the perpetual oppositions between men and women was at once made clearly apparent, and behind the conflict of the sexes, only relating to exterior facts, the gravity of the circumstances allowed the discovery of the always existent, if not always outwardly manifested fact, of the real collaboration, of the true union of these two complementary halves of humanity."

She goes on to show how easily the women have taken over most of the tasks left unoccupied by the men now at the front, and how courageous the women have proved to be at their posts. 'But where, above all, women have given proof of exceptional gifts is in their organizing faculties.' In the West 'Semitic thought allied to Roman legislation has influenced customs too deeply for women to have the opportunity of showing their capacity for organization... This is not to say that only woman's exceptional qualities have been revealed by the present war. Her weaknesses, her faults, her pettiness have also been given the opportunity of display, and certainly if women wish to take the place they claim in the governing of nations they must progress much further in the mastery of self, the broadening of ideas and points of view, in intellectual suppleness and oblivion of their sentimental preferences in order to become worthy of the management of public affairs.'

Mirra stresses the need for 'a collaboration of the two sexes ... To reduce the woman's part to solely interior and domestic occupations, and the man's part to exclusively exterior and social occupations, thus separating what should be united, would be to perpetuate the present sad state of things, from which both are

equally suffering... The question to be solved, the real question, is then not only that of a better utilization of their outer activities, but above all of an inner spiritual growth. Without inner progress there is no possible outer progress.'

Exactly when Mirra gave her talk 'To the Women of Japan' is not known. Later she found it important enough to have it reprinted several times.

Mirra had left her soul with Sri Aurobindo, who was in his physical body working out his yoga in south India. She would later say to a disciple that he was always present with her in Japan, and that he directed her stay there. Around the time that she was writing down and speaking the words quoted above, he wrote to an unknown correspondent: 'The ordinary Yoga is usually concentrated on a single aim and therefore less exposed to such recoils; ours is so complex and many-sided and embraces such large aims that we cannot expect any smooth progress until we near the completion of an effort, — especially as all the hostile forces in the spiritual world are in a constant state of opposition and besiege our gains; for the complete victory of a single one of us would mean a general downfall among them. In fact by our own effort we could not hope to succeed... The final goal is far but the progress made in the face of so constant and massive an opposition is the guarantee of its being gained in the end. But the time is in other hands than ours.'

Kyoto

For the next three years the Richards stayed mainly in the beautiful city of Kyoto, the former capital of Japan. Their close friends there were Dr. and Mrs. Kobayashi. When K.R. Srinivasa Iyengar and V.K. Gokak went to Japan in 1957, to participate in the International P.E.N. Congress, Dr. Kobayashi, a surgeon, was no longer alive, but his wife, Nobuko, received them with great courtesy and undiminished affection for her former friend Mirra. 'She came here to learn Japanese and to be one of us. But we had so much to learn from her and her charming and unpredictable ways... She revered a master from the ancient land of the Buddha... I loved her dearly. Have you seen those lovely wisteria flowers trailing down the roof of the Kasuga shrine at Nara? We call them hooji. My friend [Mirra] loved those flowers. She was one with them. She called herself Hoofiko[1] when she thought of having a Japanese name.'

Nobuko Kobayashi was by then the leader of 'The Art of Still-Sitting Movement,' founded by a certain Dr. Okata. Unhappy with the results of allopathic medicine, this doctor had made his patients sit in meditation with him and asked them to concentrate on the navel and to aspire that the Light may come down and set right the affected organ. The results were amazing. Dr. Kobayashi left his flourishing practice as a surgeon to become Okata's disciple. After the death of Dr. Kobayashi, his wife continued the movement and the meditations. The war years had been extremely difficult for the movement, but now everything was going well again and there were several thousands of practising members.

'She is the Mother to you, but always a dear, dear friend of mine,' said Nobuko Kobayashi to the two Indian writers about Mirra. 'It was my great good fortune that, in this strange but explicable world, I should have met this jewel of my heart and this friend of my soul. The perfume of those two years, when we lived like twin roses on the same stalk, lingers like incense around the divine altar and sways serenely in the sanctuary of my mind.' Later Nobuko was to meet her friend again when, in 1959, she visited India and the Sri Aurobindo Ashram in Pondicherry. 'When I see her again, I will put both my arms around her and cling to her, feeding my starved love of thirty-

---

[1] The Mother later gave names carrying their essential, spiritual meaning to many flowers. She called *Wisteria* 'poet's ecstasy,' with the comment: 'Rare and charming is your presence!'

seven long years. Will the members of your Ashram be angry with me if I behave that way? For she is now — the Mother!'

It had always been Mirra's habit to adapt to the environment in which she was moving. This time she lived the Japanese life, dressed in a kimono, as shown in several photographs, learned to speak and write the Japanese language, took a Japanese name... 'These people have a wonderful morality, live according to strict moral rules, and have a mental construction even in the least detail of life: one must eat in a certain way and not another, one must bow in a certain way and not another, one must say certain words and not other ones. When addressing certain people one must express oneself in a certain way; when speaking with others, one must express oneself in another way... Not once do you have the feeling that you are in contact with something other than a marvellously organized mental-physical domain... If one does not submit to rules there, one may live as Europeans do, who are considered barbarians and looked upon as intruders; but if you want to live a Japanese life among the Japanese you must do as they do, otherwise you make them so unhappy that you can't even have any relation with them.'

Mirra was overwhelmed by the Japanese sense of physical and natural beauty. "I had everything to learn in Japan. For four years, from an artistic point of view, I lived from wonder to wonder... From the artistic point of view, I don't think there is a country as beautiful as that." And she described the cities, then for the most part still built in the traditional Japanese style, the magnificent landscapes with their seasons of irises and flowering maples and cherries, and the artistically designed gardens, which are now imitated all over the world. "The other day I spoke to you about those landscapes of Japan. Well, almost all — the most beautiful, the most striking ones — I had seen in vision in France, and yet I had not seen any pictures or photographs of Japan, I knew nothing of Japan. And I had seen these landscapes without human beings, nothing but

the landscape, quite pure, like that, and it had seemed to me that they were visions of a world other than the physical; they seemed to me too beautiful for the physical world, too perfectly beautiful."

On April 1, 1917, Mirra wrote in her diary: 'Once more I see cherry trees everywhere; Thou hast put a magical power in these flowers; they seem to speak of Thy sole Presence; they bring with them the smile of the Divine... Japan, it is thy festive adorning, expression of thy goodwill, it is thy purest offering, the pledge of thy fidelity; it is thy way of saying that thou dost mirror the sky.' A few days later she identified with the cherry blossoms:[2] 'A deep concentration seized on me, and I perceived that I was identifying myself with a single cherry-blossom, then through it with all cherry-blossoms, and, as I descended deeper in the consciousness following a stream of bluish force, I became suddenly the cherry-tree itself, stretching towards the sky like so many arms its innumerable branches laden with their sacrifice of flowers. Then I heard distinctly this sentence: "Thus hast thou made thyself one with the soul of the cherry trees and so thou canst take note that it is the Divine who makes the offering of this flower-prayer to heaven." When I had written it, all was effaced; but now the blood of the cherry-tree flows in my veins and with it flows an incomparable peace and force.'

She started painting and drawing again, but in a style different from the paintings she had made in Paris; she was now influenced by Japanese woodblock prints. Several of those paintings and drawings have been preserved and recently reproduced in The Mother: Paintings and Drawings. Thanks to them we have an idea how Mrs. Ōkawa (Mr. Shūmei Ōkawa, 1886-1957, Japanese political activist, who supported the Freedom Movement in India) and Nobuko Kobayashi looked,

---

[2] The epistemological problem is central to the whole of Western philosophy. The Mother and Sri Aurobindo's answer to it is that one can know something that is not oneself only by identification.

as well as the poet Hirasawa Tetsuo, whom she painted at one sitting and about whom little or nothing is known, and the poet Hayashi, who is still more mysterious. She also painted or drew some of the places she visited — among them the Daiunji temple — and people she met, such as Rabindranath Tagore. 'The art of Japan is a kind of directly mental expression in physical life. The Japanese use the vital world very little. Their art is extremely mentalized; their life is extremely mentalized. It expresses in detail quite precise mental formations. Only, in the physical do they have spontaneously the sense of beauty.

'It was a Japanese street brilliantly illuminated by gay lanterns picturesquely adorned with vivid colours. And as gradually what was conscious [i.e. Mirra herself] moved on down the street, the Divine appeared, visible in everyone and everything. One of the lightly-built houses became transparent, revealing a woman seated on a tatami in a sumptuous violet kimono embroidered with gold and bright colours. The woman was beautiful and must have been between thirty-five and forty. She was playing a golden saniisen. At her feet lay a little child. And in the woman too the Divine was visible.' This exquisite cameo of life in Japan was noted down by Mirra in her diary on 5 December 1916. The reader may recall Sri Aurobindo's realization of the cosmic consciousness when he saw Lord Krishna in all the people and objects of Alipore jail. Mirra must have had the same consciousness at least since her identification with the Great Mother.

V.K. Gokak has recorded some of his conversations with Shumei Okawa and Nobuko Kobayashi in a beautiful poetic form, but poetry in a context like this often comes closer to the truth than ordinary prose. The following words, attributed to Shumei Okawa, are well-known but bear repetition here: 'You would like to know, my young friend, what struck me about your Mother. She had a will that moved the mountains and an intellect sharp as the edge of a sword. Her thought was clarity itself and her resolve stronger than the roots of a giant oak. Her mystic depths were deeper than the ocean, but her intellect was a plummet that could sound her deepest depths. An artist, she could paint pictures of an unearthly loveliness. A musician, she enchanted my soul when she played on an organ or guitar. A scientist, she could formulate a new Heaven and Earth, a new cosmogony. I do not know what Mirra had not become or was not capable of becoming.'

Towards the end of the war there was a severe pandemic of 'Spanish flu' which killed more than twenty million people, more than fell in the war itself. The pandemic raged also in Japan. The Mother told how a little village had been attacked by it without anybody outside the village knowing, for it was wintertime, the countryside was covered with snow and the village was isolated. When a letter was sent to one of the villagers, the postman who took it found no sign of life any more in the village; all had died and the snow was their common shroud.

Mirra herself had a close call. 'I was in Japan. It was at the beginning of January 1919. It was the time that a terrible flu raged in the whole of Japan which killed hundreds of thousands of people. It was one of those epidemics the like of which are rarely seen. In Tokyo there were hundreds and hundreds of new cases every day. The disease... lasted three days and on the third day the patient died... If one did not die on the third day, at the end of seven days one was altogether cured...

'It so happened that I was living with somebody [Paul Richard] who never ceased troubling me: "But what is this disease? What is there behind this disease?" What I was doing, you know, was simply to cover myself with my force, my protection, so as not to catch it and I did not think of it any more and went along doing my work... But constantly I had to hear: "What is this? I would like to know what is there behind this illness. Could you not tell me what this illness is, why it is there?" Etcetera.

'One day I was called to the other end of the town by a young woman whom I knew and who wanted to introduce me to some friends and show me certain things... I had to cross the whole city in a tramcar. And I was in the tram and saw all those people with masks on their noses, and there was in the atmosphere that constant fear, and so there came a suggestion to me — I began to ask myself: "Actually what is this illness? What is there behind this illness? What are the forces that are in this illness?"... I returned home with a terrible fever. I had caught it...'

Mirra refused the medicine given to her by the doctor called to her bed. 'At the end of the second day, as I was lying all alone, I saw clearly a being with a part of the head cut off, in a military uniform — or what remained of a military uniform — approaching me and suddenly flinging himself upon my chest, with that half head, to suck my force. I took a good look, then realized that I was about to die. He was drawing my life out... I was completely nailed to the bed, without any movement, in deep trance. I could not stir and he was pulling. I thought: "This is the end." Then I called on my occult power, I gave a big fight and I succeeded in pushing him off so that he could not stay any longer. And I woke up...

'I had understood that the illness originated from beings who had been thrown violently out of their bodies. I had seen this during the First World War, towards the end, when people were staying in trenches and were killed in bombardments. They were in perfect health, altogether healthy, and in the blink of an eye they were thrown out of their bodies, not conscious that they were dead. They didn't know that they had no body any more and tried to find in others the life force they could not find in themselves. Which means that they had become so many countless vampires. And they vampirized upon human beings... I know how much knowledge and force were necessary for me to resist. It was irresistible [for ordinary persons]'.

Then Mirra asked to be left alone for a couple of days, concentrated on the evil that was sucking the life out of so many humans, and put things straight. At the end of two or three days there was no longer a single case of illness in the city.

With the help of the Japanese Government, and in spite of British protests, the Richards obtained their travel documents and left in 1920 for Pondicherry.

Text extracted from George Van Vrekhem's book
'The Mother – The Story of Her Life.'

Impressions of Japan

You ask me for my impressions about Japan. To write on Japan is a difficult task; so many things have been already written, so many silly things also.., but these more on the people than on their country. For the country is so wonderful, picturesque, many-sided, unexpected, charming, wild or sweet; it is in its appearance so much a synthesis of all the other countries of the world, from the tropical to the arctic, that no artistic eye can remain indifferent to it. I believe many excellent descriptions have been given of Japan; I shall not then attempt to add mine, which would certainly be far less interesting. But the people of Japan have, in general, been misunderstood and misinterpreted, and on that subject something worth saying remains to be said.

In most cases foreigners come in touch with that part of the Japanese people which has been spoiled by foreigners, — a Japan of money-makers and imitators of the West; obviously they have proved very clever imitators, and you can easily find here a great many of those things which make the West hateful. If we judge Japan by her statesmen, her politicians and her businessmen, we shall find her a country very much like one of the Powers of Europe, though she possesses the vitality and concentrated energies of a nation which has not yet reached its zenith.

That energy is one of the most interesting features of Japan. It is visible everywhere, in everyone; the old and the young, the workmen, the women, the children, the students, all, save perhaps the "new rich", display in their daily life the most wonderful storage of concentrated energy. With their perfect love for nature and beauty, this accumulated strength is, perhaps, the most distinctive and widely spread characteristic of the Japanese. That is what you may observe as soon as you reach that land of the Rising Sun, where so many people and so many treasures are gathered in a narrow Island.

But if you have — as we have had — the privilege of coming in contact with the true Japanese, those who kept untouched the righteousness and bravery of the ancient Samurai, then you can understand what in truth is Japan, you can seize the secret of her force. They know how to remain silent; and though they are possessed of the most acute sensitiveness, they are, among the people I have met, those who express it the least. A friend here can give his life with the greatest simplicity to save yours, though he never told you before he loved you in such a profound and unselfish way. Indeed he had not even told you that he had loved you at all. And if you were not able to read the heart behind the appearances, you would have seen only a very exquisite courtesy which leaves little room for the expression of spontaneous feelings. Nevertheless the feelings are there, all the stronger perhaps because of the lack of outward manifestation; and if an opportunity presents itself, through an act, very modest and veiled sometimes, you suddenly discover depths of affection.

This is specifically Japanese; among the nations of the world, the true Japanese — those who have not become westernized — are perhaps the least selfish. And this unselfishness is not the privilege of the well-educated, the learned or the religious people; in all social ranks you may find it. For here, with the exception of some popular and exceedingly pretty festivals,

religion is not a rite or a cult, it is a daily life of abnegation, obedience, self-sacrifice.

The Japanese are taught from their infancy that life is duty and not pleasure. They accept that duty — so often hard and painful — with passive submission. They are not tormented by the idea of making themselves happy. It gives to the life of the whole country a very remarkable self-constraint, but no joyful and free expansion; it creates an atmosphere of tension and effort, of mental and nervous strain, not of spiritual peace like that which can be felt in India, for instance. Indeed, nothing in Japan can be compared to the pure divine atmosphere which pervades India and makes of her such a unique and precious country; not even in the temples and the sacred monasteries always so wonderfully situated, sometimes on the summit of a high mountain covered with huge cedar trees, difficult to reach, far from the world below.... Exterior calm, rest and silence are there, but not that blissful sense of the infinite which comes from a living nearness to the Unique. True, here all speaks to the eyes and mind of unity — unity of God with man, unity of man with Nature, unity of man with man. But this unity is very little felt and lived. Certainly the Japanese have a highly developed sense of generous hospitality, reciprocal help, mutual support; but in their feelings, their thoughts, their actions in general, they are among the most individualist, the most separatist people. For them the form is predominant, the form is attractive. It is suggestive too, it speaks of some deeper harmony or truth, of some law of nature or life. Each form, each act is symbolical, from the arrangement of the gardens and the houses to the famous tea ceremony. And sometimes in a very simple and usual thing you discover a symbol, deep, elaborated, willed, that most of the people know and understand; but it is an exterior and learnt knowledge — a tradition, it is not living truth coming from the depth of spiritual experience, enlightening heart and mind. Japan is essentially the country of sensations; she lives through her eyes. Beauty rules over her as an uncontested master; and all her atmosphere incites to mental and vital activity, study, observation, progress, effort, not to silent and blissful contemplation. But behind this activity stands a high aspiration which the future of her people will reveal.

Words of Long Ago

On Japanese Art

What is the difference between Japanese art and the art of other countries, like those of Europe, for example?

The art of Japan is a kind of directly mental expression in physical life. The Japanese use the vital world very little. Their art is extremely mentalised; their life is extremely mentalised. It expresses in detail quite precise mental formations. Only, in the physical, they have spontaneously the sense of beauty. For example, a thing one sees very rarely in Europe but constantly, daily in Japan: very simple people, men of the working class or even peasants go for rest or enjoyment to a place where they can see a beautiful landscape. This gives them a much greater joy than going to play cards or indulging in all sorts of distractions as they do in the countries of Europe. They are seen in groups at times, going on the roads or sometimes taking a train or a tram up to a certain point, then walking to a place from where one gets a beautiful view. Then at this place there is a small house which fits very well into the landscape, there is a kind of small platform on which one can sit: one takes a cup of tea and at the same time sees the landscape. For them, this is the supreme enjoyment; they

In the world of forms a flaw in Beauty

is as great a deficiency

as a flaw in Truth in the world of Ideas.

The Mother, 1969

know nothing more pleasant. One can understand this among artists, educated people, quite learned people, but I am speaking of people of the most ordinary class, poor people who like this better than resting or relaxing at home. This is for them the greatest joy.

And in that country, for each season there are known sites. For instance, in autumn leaves become red; they have large numbers of maple-trees (the leaves of the maple turn into all the shades of the most vivid red in autumn, it is absolutely marvellous), so they arrange a place near a temple, for instance, on the top of a hill, and the entire hill is covered with maples.

There is a stairway which climbs straight up, almost like a ladder, from the base to the top, and it is so steep that one cannot see what is at the top, one gets the feeling of a ladder rising to the skies — a stone stairway, very well made, rising steeply and seeming to lose itself in the sky — clouds pass, and both the sides of the hill are covered with maples, and these maples have the most magnificent colours you could ever imagine. Well, an artist who goes there will experience an emotion of absolutely exceptional, marvellous beauty. But one sees very small children, families even, with a baby on the shoulder, going there in groups. In autumn they will go there. In springtime they will go elsewhere.

There is a garden quite close to Tokyo where irises are grown, a garden with very tiny rivulets, and along the rivulets, irises — irises of all possible colours — and it is arranged according to colour, organised in such a way that on entering one is dazzled, there is a blaze of colour from all these flowers standing upright; and there are heaps and heaps of them, as far as the eye can reach. At another time, just at the beginning of spring (it is a slightly early spring there), there are the first cherry-trees. These cherry-trees never give fruit, they are grown only for the flowers. They range from white to pink, to a rather vivid pink. There are long avenues all bordered with cherry-trees, all pink; they are huge trees which have turned all pink.

There are entire mountains covered with these cherry-trees, and on the little rivulets bridges have been built which too are all red: you see these bridges of red lacquer among all these pink flowers and, below, a great river flowing and a mountain which seems to scale the sky, and they go to this place in springtime... For each season there are flowers and for each flower there are gardens.

And people travel by train as easily as one goes from house to house; they have a small packet like this which they carry; in it they have a change of clothes, that's quite enough for them; they wear on the feet rope or fibre sandals; when these get worn out they throw them away and take others, for it costs nothing at all. All their life is like that. They have paper handkerchiefs, when they have used them they get rid of them, and so on — they don't burden themselves with anything. When they go by train, at the stations small meals are sold in boxes (it is quite clean, quite neat), small meals in boxes of white wood with little chopsticks for eating; then, as all this has no value, when one has finished, one puts them aside, doesn't bother about them or encumber oneself. They live like that. When they have a garden or a park, they plant trees, and they plant them just at the place where when the tree has grown it will create a landscape, will fit into a landscape. And as they want the tree to have a particular shape, they trim it, cut it, they manage to give it all the shapes they want. You have trees with fantastic forms; they have cut off the unnecessary branches, fostered others, contrived things as they liked. Then you come to a place and you see a house which seems to be altogether a part of the landscape; it has exactly the right colour, it is made of the right materials; it is not like a blow in your face, as are all those European buildings which spoil the whole landscape. It is just there where it should be, hidden under the trees; then you see a creeper and suddenly a wonderful tree; it is there at the right place, it has the right form. I had everything to learn in Japan. For four years, from an artistic point of view, I lived from wonder to wonder.

And in the cities, a city like Tokyo, for example, which is the biggest city in the world, bigger than London, and which extends far, far (now the houses are modernised, the whole centre of the city is very unpleasant, but when I was there, it was still good), in the outlying parts of the city, those which are not business quarters, every house has at the most two storeys and a garden — there is always a garden, there are always one or two trees which are quite lovely. And then, if you go for a walk... it is very difficult to find your way in Tokyo; there are no straight streets with houses on either side according to the number, and you lose your way easily. Then you go wandering around — always one wanders at random in that country — you go wandering and all of a sudden you turn the corner of a street and come to a kind of paradise: there are magnificent trees, a temple as beautiful as everything else, you see nothing of the city any longer, no more traffic, no tramways; a corner, a corner of trees with magnificent colours, and it is beautiful, beautiful like everything else. You do not know how you have reached there, you seem to have come by luck. And then you turn, you seek your way, you wander off again and go elsewhere. And some days later you want to come back to this very place, but it is impossible, it is as though it had disappeared. And this is so frequent, this is so true that such stories are often told in Japan. Their literature is full of fairy-lore. They tell you a story in which the hero comes suddenly to an enchanted place: he sees fairies, he sees marvellous beings, he spends exquisite hours among flowers, music; all is splendid. The next day he is obliged to leave; it is the law of the place, he goes away. He tries to come back, but never does. He can no longer find the place: it was there, it has disappeared!... And everything in this city, in this country, from beginning to end, gives you the impression of impermanence, of the unexpected, the exceptional. You always come to things you did not expect; you want to find them again and they are lost – they have made something else which is equally charming. From the artistic point of view, the point of view of beauty, I don't think there is a country as beautiful as that.

Now, I ought to say, to complete my picture, that the four years I was there I found a dearth of spirituality as entire as could be. These people have a wonderful morality, live according to quite strict moral rules, they have a mental construction even in the least detail of life: one must eat in a certain way and not another, one must bow in a certain way and not another, one must say certain words but not all; when addressing certain people one must express oneself in a certain way; when speaking with others, one must express oneself in another. If you go to buy something in a shop, you must say a particular sentence; if you don't say it, you are not served: they look at you quizzically and do not move! But if you say the word, they wait upon you with full attention and bring, if necessary, a cushion for you to sit upon and a cup of tea to drink. And everything is like that. However, not once do you have the feeling that you are in contact with something other than a marvellously organised mental-physical domain. And what energy they have! Their whole vital being is turned into energy. They have an extraordinary endurance but no direct aspiration: one must obey the rule, one is obliged. If one does not submit oneself to rules there, one may live as Europeans do, who are considered barbarians and looked upon altogether as intruders, but if you want to live a Japanese life among the Japanese you must do as they do, otherwise you make them so unhappy that you can't even have any relation with them. In their house you must live in a particular way, when you meet them you must greet them in a particular way... I think I have already told you the story of that Japanese who was an intimate friend of ours, and whom I helped to come into contact with his soul — and who ran away. He was in the countryside with us and I had put him in touch with his psychic being; he had the experience, a revelation, the contact, the dazzling inner contact. And the next morning, he was no longer there, he had taken flight! Later, when I saw him again in town after the holidays, I asked him, "But what happened to you, why did you go away?" — "Oh! you understand, I discovered my soul and saw that my soul was more powerful than my faith in the country and the Mikado; I would have had to obey my soul and I would no longer have been a faithful subject of my emperor. I had to go away." There you are! All this is authentically true.

Questions and Answers, 12 April 1951

THE 1919 FLU IN JAPAN

I was in Japan. It was at the beginning of January 1919. Anyway, it was the time when a terrible flu raged there in the whole of Japan, which killed hundreds of thousands of people. It was one of those epidemics the like of which is rarely seen. In Tokyo, every day there were hundreds and hundreds of new cases. The disease appeared to take this turn: it lasted three days and on the third day the patient died. And people died in such large numbers that they could not even be cremated, you understand, it was impossible, there were too many of them. Or otherwise, if one did not die on the third day, at the end of seven days one was altogether cured; a little exhausted but all the same completely cured. There was a panic in the town, for epidemics are very rare in Japan. They are a very clean people, very careful and with a fine morale. Illnesses are very rare. But still this came, it came as a catastrophe. There was a terrible fear. For example, people were seen walking about in the streets with a mask on the nose, a mask to purify the air they were breathing, so that it might not be full of the microbes of the illness. It was a common fear... Now, it so happened I was living with someone who never ceased troubling me: "But what is this disease? What is there behind this disease?"

What I was doing, you know, was simply to cover myself with my force, my protection so as not to catch it and I did not think of it any more and continued doing my work. Nothing happened and I was not thinking of it. But constantly I heard: "What is this? Oh. I would like to know what is there behind this illness. But could you not tell me what this illness is, why it is there?..." etc. One day I was called to the other end of the town by a young woman whom I knew and who wished to introduce me to some friends and show me certain things: I do not remember now what exactly was the matter, but anyway I had to cross the whole town in a tram-car. And I was in the tram and seeing these people with masks on their noses, and then there was in the atmosphere this constant fear, and so there came a suggestion to me; I began to ask myself: "Truly, what is this illness? What is there behind this illness? What are the forces that are in this illness?..." I came to the house, I passed an hour there and I returned. And I returned with a terrible fever. I had caught it. It came to you thus, without preparation, instantaneously. Illnesses, generally illnesses from germs and microbes, take a few days in the system: they come, there is a little battle inside; you win or you lose, if you lose you catch the illness, it is not complicated. But there, you just receive a letter, open the envelope, hop! puff! The next minute you have the fever. Well, that evening I had a terrible fever. The doctor was called (it was not I who called him), the doctor was called and he told me: "I must absolutely give you this medicine." It was one of the best medicines for the fever, he had just a little (all their stocks were exhausted, everyone was taking it); he said: "I have still a few packets, I shall give you some"— "I beg of you, do not give it to me, I won't take it. Keep it for someone who has faith in it and will take it." He was quite disgusted: "It was no use my coming here." So I said: "Perhaps it was no use!" And I remained in my bed, with my fever, a violent fever. All the while I was asking myself: "What is this illness? Why is it there? What is there behind it?..." At the end of the second day, as I was lying all alone, I saw clearly a being, with a part of the head cut off, in a military uniform (or the remains of a military uniform) approaching me and suddenly flinging himself upon my chest, with that half a head to suck my force. I took a good look, then realised that I was about to die. He was drawing all my life out (for I must tell you that people were dying of pneumonia in three days). I was completely nailed to the bed, without movement, in a deep trance. I could no longer stir and he was pulling. I thought: now it is the end. Then I called on my occult power, I gave a big fight and I succeeded in turning him back so that he could not stay there any longer. And I woke up.

But I had seen. And I had learnt, I had understood that the illness originated from beings who had been thrown out of their bodies. I had seen this during the First Great War, towards its end, when people used to live in trenches and were killed by bombardment. They were in perfect health, altogether healthy, and in a second they were thrown out of their bodies, not conscious that they were dead. They did not know they hadn't a body any more and they tried to find in others the life they could not find in themselves. That is, they were turned into so many countless vampires. And they vampirised upon men. And then over and above that, there was a decomposition of the vital forces of people who fell ill and died. One lived in a kind of sticky and thick cloud made up of all that. And so those who took in this cloud fell ill and usually got cured, but those who were attacked by a being of that kind invariably died, they could not resist. I know how much knowledge and force were necessary for me to resist. It was irresistible. That is, if they were attacked by a being who was a centre of this whirl of bad forces, they died. And there must have been many of these, a very great number. I saw all that and I understood.

When someone came to see me, I asked to be left alone, I lay quietly in my bed and I passed two or three days absolutely quiet, in concentration, with my consciousness. Subsequently, a friend of ours (a Japanese, a very good friend) came and told me: "Ah! you were ill? So what I thought was true... Just imagine for the last two or three days, there hasn't been a single new case of illness in the town and most of the people who were ill have been cured and the number of deaths has become almost negligible, and now it is all over. The illness is wholly under control." Then I narrated what had happened to me and he went and narrated it to everybody. They even published articles about it in the papers.

Well, consciousness, to be sure, is more effective than packets of medicine!... The condition was critical. Just imagine, there were entire villages where everyone had died. There was a village in Japan, not very big, but still with more than a hundred people, and it happened, due to an extraordinary chance, that one of the villagers was to receive a letter (the postman went there only if there was a letter; naturally, it was a village far in the countryside); so he went to the countryside; there was a snowfall; the whole village was under snow... and there was not a living person. It was exactly so. It was that kind of epidemic. And Tokyo was also like that; but Tokyo was a big town and things did not happen in the same fashion. And it was in this way the epidemic ended. That is my story.

Question and Answers, 22 July 1953

The 1918 flu pandemic (commonly referred to as the Spanish Flu) was an influenza pandemic that spread to nearly every part of the world. It was caused by an unusually virulent and deadly influenza, a virus strain of subtype H1N1. Historical and epidemiological data are inadequate to identify the geographic origin of the virus. Most of its victims were healthy young adults, in contrast to most influenza outbreaks which predominantly affect juvenile, elderly, or otherwise weakened patients. The flu pandemic has also been implicated in the sudden outbreak of encephalitis lethargica in the 1920s.

The pandemic lasted from March 1918 to June 1920, spreading even to the Arctic and remote Pacific islands. It is estimated that anywhere from 50 to 100 million people were killed worldwide, which is from three to seven times the casualties of the First World War (15 million), making it the most deadly natural disaster in human history. An estimated 50 million people, about 3% of the world's population (approximately 1.6 billion at the time), died of the disease. An estimated 500 million, or 1/3 were infected.

The global mortality rate from the 1918/1919 pandemic is not known, but it is estimated that 10% to 20% of those who were infected died. With about a third of the world population infected, this case-fatality ratio means that 3% to 6% of the entire global population died. Influenza may have killed as many as 25 million in its first 25 weeks. Older estimates say it killed 40–50 million people, while current estimates say 50—100 million people worldwide were killed. This pandemic has been described as "the greatest medical holocaust in history" and may have killed more people than the Black Death.

As many as 17 million died in India, about 5% of India's population at the time. In Japan, 23 million people were affected, and 390,000 died.

Wikipedia, encyclopedia

. . . There are some strange things. When I went to Japan, I met a man there who was a striking reproduction of my father—the first moment, I wondered if I was dreaming. I think my father was already dead, but I am not sure, I don't remember exactly (my father died while I was in Japan, that's all I know). But he was the same age as my father, which means they were born together, at the same time. My father was born in Turkey, while this one was born in Japan—but anyway, it WAS my father! And this man took to me with a paternal passion, it was extraordinary! He wanted to see me all the time, he showered me with gifts.... And we could hardly talk to each other, as he knew very little English. But what a resemblance! As if one were the exact replica of the other: same size, same features, same colour (he was exceptionally white for a Japanese, and my father wasn't white as northern people are: he was white as people from the Middle East are, just like me).

It always surprised me. You know, people often say, "Oh, they look like each other," but that's not it! He was like an exact replica.

But inwardly too, occultly too?

There was a kind of affinity.

He was an inventive man—my father also had a very inventive imagination. But my father was a first-rate mathematician, while I don't know about this man.... He had invented a "meditating machine"! It was really very interesting, I even brought it back; it worked with batteries and I couldn't replace them, so it's useless now. It must still be around somewhere. But it's a machine like the prayer wheel, something of that sort, but it was a "meditating machine"! It was very interesting.

There are some strange things. ...

Mother Aganda, August 8, 1964

The Children of Japan

In my last letter[3] I spoke of the sense of duty which gave to the Japanese people a great self-constraint, but no joyful and free expansion. I must make an exception to this rule and this exception is in favour of the children.

We could quite well call Japan the paradise of children — in no other country I have seen them so free and so happy. After months of residence in Japan I have yet never seen a child beaten by a grown-up person. They are treated as if all the parents were conscious that the children are the promise and the glory of the future. And a wonderful thing is that, environed by so much attention, so much care, — indeed, such a devotion, they are the most reasonable, good and serious children I have ever met. When they are babies, tied up in an amusing fashion on their mothers' backs, with their wide open black eyes they seem to consider life with gravity and to have already opinions on the things they look at. You scarcely hear a child cry. When, for instance, he has hurt himself and the tears burst out of his eyes, the mother or the father has but to say a few words in a low voice, and the sorrow seems to be swept away. What are those magic words which enable children to be

---

[3] i.e. "Impressions of Japan".

so reasonable? Very simple indeed: "Are you not a Samurai?" And this question is sufficient for the child to call to him all his energy and to overcome his weakness.

In the streets you see hundreds of children, in their charming bright *"kimono"*,[4] playing freely, in spite of the *"kuruma"*[5] and the bicycles, at the most inventive and picturesque games, pleased with little, singing and laughing.

When older, but still very young, you may see them in the tram cars, dressed with foreign clothes, the student cap on the head, the knapsack on the back, proud of their importance, still prouder at the idea of all they are learning and will learn. For they love their studies and are the most earnest students. They never miss an opportunity of adding something to their growing knowledge; and when the work for the school leaves them some liberty they occupy it in reading books. The young Japanese seem to have a real passion for books. In Tokyo one of the main streets is nearly entirely occupied by secondhand book-sellers. From the beginning to the end of the year these shops are full of students, and it is not often novels they are seeking for!

They are, as a rule, very anxious to learn foreign languages, and when they come to meet foreigners, though they are in general very timid, they make use of that acquaintance as much as they can to...[6]

A country where such are the children and so they are treated as a country still ascending the steps of progress and of mastery.

Words of Long Ago

---

[4] Traditional wide-sleeved gown.

[5] A word applied to many vehicles, here probably a carriage or a rickshaw.

[6] This sentence was left incomplete.

To the Women of Japan

To speak of children to the women of Japan is, I think, to speak to them of their dearest, their most sacred subject. Indeed, in no other country in the world have the children taken such an important, such a primordial place. They are, here, the centre of care and attention. On them are concentrated — and rightly — the hopes for the future. They are the living promise of growing prosperity for the country. Therefore, the most important work assigned to women in Japan is child-making. Maternity is considered as the principal role of woman. But this is true only so long as we understand what is meant by the word maternity. For to bring children into the world as rabbits do their young — instinctively, ignorantly, machine-like, that certainly cannot be called maternity! True maternity begins with the conscious creation of a being, with the willed shaping of a soul coming to develop and utilise a new body. The true domain of women is the spiritual. We forget it but too often.

To bear a child and construct his body almost subconsciously is not enough. The work really commences when, by the power of thought and will, we conceive and create a character capable of manifesting an ideal.

And do not say that we have no power for realising such a thing. Innumerable instances of this very effective power could be brought out as proofs.

First of all, the effect of physical environment was recognised and studied long ago. It is by surrounding women with forms of art and beauty that, little by little, the ancient Greeks created the exceptionally harmonious race that they were.

Individual instances of the same fact are numerous. It is not rare to see a woman who, while pregnant, had looked at constantly and admired a beautiful picture or statue, giving birth to a child after the perfect likeness of this picture or statue. I met several of these instances myself. Among them, I remember very clearly two little girls; they were twins and perfectly beautiful. But the most astonishing was how little like their parents they were. They reminded me of a very famous picture painted by the English artist Reynolds. One day I made this remark to the mother, who immediately exclaimed: "Indeed, is it not so? You will be interested to know that while I was expecting these children, I had, hanging above my bed, a very good reproduction of Reynolds' picture. Before going to sleep and as soon as I woke, my last and first glance was for that picture; and in my heart I hoped: may my children be like the faces in this picture. You see that I succeeded quite well!" In truth, she could be proud of her success, and her example is of great utility for other women.

But if we can obtain such results on the physical plane where the materials are the least plastic, how much more so on the psychological plane where the influence of thought and will is so powerful. Why accept the obscure bonds of heredity and atavism — which are nothing else than subconscious preferences for our own trend of character — when we can, by concentration and will, call into being a type constructed according to the highest ideal we are able to conceive? With this effort, maternity becomes truly precious and sacred;

indeed with this, we enter the glorious work of the Spirit, and womanhood rises above animality and its ordinary instincts, towards real humanity and its powers.

In this effort, in this attempt, then, lies our true duty. And if this duty was always of the greatest importance, it certainly has taken a capital one in the present turn of the earth's evolution.

For we are living in an exceptional time at an exceptional turning point of the world's history. Never before, perhaps, did mankind pass through such a dark period of hatred, bloodshed and confusion. And, at the same time, never had such a strong, such an ardent hope awakened in the hearts of the people. Indeed, if we listen to our heart's voice, we immediately perceive that we are, more or less consciously, waiting for a new reign of justice, of beauty, of harmonious good-will and fraternity. And this seems in complete contradiction with the actual state of the world. But we all know that never is the night so dark as before the dawn. May not this darkness, then, be the sign of an approaching dawn? And as never was night so complete, so terrifying, maybe never will dawn have been so bright, so pure, so illuminating as the coming one.... After the bad dreams of the night the world will awaken to a new consciousness.

The civilization which is ending now in such a dramatic way was based on the power of mind, mind dealing with matter and life. What it has been to the world, we have not to discuss here. But a new reign is coming, that of the Spirit: after the human, the divine.

Yet, if we have been fortunate enough to live on earth at such a stupendous, a unique time as this one, is it sufficient to stand and watch the unfolding events? All those who feel that their heart extends further than the limits of their own person and family, that their thought embraces more than small personal interests and local conventions, all those, in short, who realise that they belong not to themselves, or to their family, or even to their country, but to God who manifests Himself in all countries, through mankind, these, indeed, know that they must rise and set to work for the sake of humanity, for the advent of the Dawn.

And in this momentous, endless, many-sided work, what can be the part of womanhood? It is true that, as soon as great events and works are in question, the custom is to relegate women to a corner with a smile of patronising contempt which means: this is not your business, poor, feeble, futile creatures... And women, submissive, childlike, lazy perhaps, have accepted, at least in many countries, this deplorable state of things. I dare to say that they are wrong. In the life of the future, there shall be no more room for such division, such disequilibrium between the masculine and the feminine. The true relation of the two sexes is an equal footing of mutual help and close collaboration.

And from now, we must reassume our veritable position, take again our due place and assert our real importance— that of spiritual former and educator. Indeed, some men, perhaps a little vainglorious of their so-called advantages, may despise the apparent weakness of women (although even this exterior weakness is not quite certain) but: "Do what he may, the superman will have to be born of woman all the same," someone said very rightly.

The superman shall be born of woman, this is a big unquestionable truth; but it is not enough to be proud of this truth, we must clearly understand what it means, become aware of the responsibility it creates, and learn to face earnestly the task which is put before us. This task is precisely our most important share in the present world-wide work.

For that, we must first understand — at least in their broad lines, what are the means by which the present chaos and obscurity can be transformed into light and harmony.

Many means have been suggested: political, social, ethical, even religious.... Indeed, none of these seem sufficient to face with any reliable success the magnitude of the task to be done. Only a new spiritual influx, creating in man a new consciousness, can overcome the enormous mass of difficulties barring the way of the workers. A new spiritual light, a manifestation upon earth of some divine force unknown until now, a Thought of God, new for us, descending into this world and taking a new form here.

And here we come back to our starting point, to our duty of true maternity. For this form meant to manifest the spiritual force capable of transforming the earth's present conditions, this new form, who is to construct it if not the women?

Thus we see that at this critical period of the world's life it is no longer sufficient to give birth to a being in whom our highest personal ideal is manifested; we must strive to find out what is the future type, whose advent Nature is planning. It is no longer sufficient to form a man similar to the greatest men we have heard of or known, or even greater, more accomplished and gifted than they; we must strive to come in touch mentally, by the constant aspiration of our thought and will, with the supreme possibility which, exceeding all human measures and features, will give birth to the superman.

Once again Nature feels one of her great impulses towards the creation of something utterly new, something unexpected. And it is to this impulse that we must answer and obey.

Let us try first to discover where this impulse of Nature will lead us. And the best way for that is to look back on the lessons given to us by the Past.

We see that each progress of Nature, each manifestation of a new capacity and principle upon earth is marked by the appearance of a new species. In the same way, the progressive forms of the life of races, of peoples, of individuals, follow each other through the human cycles, ceaselessly inspired, fecundated, renewed by the efforts of the guides of humanity.

And all these forms aim at the same goal, the mysterious, the glorious goal of Nature.[7]

---

[7] It seems that the following paragraphs from an earlier draft were intended for insertion here:

Which is this goal? Toward what unexpected realisation of the future does Nature aim? What does she seek since her dark origins?

Each form that she creates is a fresh affirmation of that which through her will be born, of that which it is her mission to manifest.

Each species preparing the others, making them possible, bears witness to her untiring perseverance, is a proof of her solemn vow; in each one is a little more matter transfigured, announcing future dawns of intelligence. Through innumerable cycles how many paths has she had to follow in order to reach at last the cave of the anthropoid, the primitive man?

It is before him that will open the royal avenue leading to the palace of spirit. But how many races, how many generations will pass on the earth without discovering it, how many wrong paths will Nature follow in the footsteps of man. For, believing himself the masterpiece of the universe he knows not that he has a further stage to pass through.

Could the idea of man be conceived, before he existed, in the obscure brain of even the nearest of his ancestors? Can the idea of the superman, before he exists, penetrate into the brain of man?

And yet, in every child of man which comes into the world, in every growing intelligence, in every effort of the emerging generations, in every attempt of human genius, Nature seeks the way which, once again, will lead her further.

Fifteen hundred million men since perhaps fifteen hundred centuries wander without finding this way.

Among the multitude of the ways over which all the efforts of their progress are scattered, in this domain as in all the others, only one is good: it is the way of synthetic perfections. Where to discover it?

And who among men dares to venture elsewhere than on the easy and well-beaten tracks? Who, knowing that there is another path which goes further, accepts to lose all in order to find it perhaps, to lose all in walking alone, in thinking alone, always apart among the others, not even certain of attaining what he seeks.

Try not to discover this one among the men who excel and shine, for these excel and shine only in being, somewhat more perfectly, similar to their own kind.

Precious stones also excel and shine among all the other stones, but the most beautiful gem is outside the series of chemical combinations from whence comes forth life. In the same way, ascending the series of forms, the most beautiful tree of the forest is outside the lines of evolution which lead the biological process up to the animal, up to man.

And once again, among men, the most admired, the most famous, the most artistic, the most learned, the most religious, may well find himself far off the way leading from man to superman.

Each race, each civilization, each human society, each religion, represents a new attempt of Nature, one more effort adding to the long series of those she multiplied during countless time.

Now, as among all the animal forms there was one from which man was to come forth, so also, among the social and religious species, must one be born from which some day

It is to this call of Nature that we must answer, to this magnificent, to this grandiose work that we must devote ourselves. Let us try to make as clear as we can the steps of our advance on this difficult and as yet unexplored path.

First of all we must be careful, in our attempt to conceive the future man or superman, not to adopt an actual type of man, perfecting or aggrandising him. To avoid as much as possible this mistake we should study the teachings of life's evolution.

We have already seen that the appearance of a new species always announces the manifestation on earth of a new principle, a new plane of consciousness, a new force or power. But, at the same time, while the new species acquires this formerly unmanifested power or consciousness, it may lose one or many of the perfections which were the characteristics of the immediately preceding species. For instance, to speak only of the last step of Nature's development, what are the greatest differences between man and his immediate predecessor, the ape? In the monkey we see vitality and physical ability reaching the utmost perfection, a perfection that the new species had to abandon. For man, there has been no more of that marvellous climbing up trees, somersaults over abysses, jumps from summit to summit, but in exchange he acquired intelligence, the power of reasoning, combining, constructing. Indeed with man it is the life of mind, of intellect which appeared on earth. Man is essentially a mental being; and if his possibilities do not stop there, if he feels in himself other worlds, other faculties, other planes of consciousness beyond his mental life, they are only as promises for the future, in the same way as the mental possibilities are latent in the monkey.

---

will come forth the superman.

For it is this which Nature seeks in all her successive attempts, from the first germination of life until man, until the God who shall be born of him.

In the multitude of men she seeks the possibility of the superman; and in each one of them, she aims towards the realisation of the divine.

It is true that some men, very few, have lived in that world beyond, which we may call the spiritual; some have been, indeed, the living incarnations of that world on earth, but they are the exceptions, the forerunners showing the way to the race, leading it towards its future realisation, not the average man. But that which was the privilege of a few beings scattered through time and space, shall become the central characteristic of the new type which is to appear.

At present, man governs his life through reason; all the activities of the mind are of common use for him; his means of knowledge are observation and deduction; it is by and through reasoning that he takes his decision and chooses his way — or believes he does — in life.

The new race shall be governed by intuition, that is to say, direct perception of the divine law within. Some human beings actually know and experience intuition — as, undoubtedly, certain big gorillas of the forests have glimpses of reasoning.

In mankind, the very few who have cultivated their inner self, who have concentrated their energies on the discovery of the true law of their being, possess more or less the faculty of intuition. When the mind is perfectly silent, pure like a well-polished mirror, immobile as a pond on a breezeless day, then, from above, as the light of the stars drops in the motionless waters, so the light of the supermind, of the Truth within, shines in the quieted mind and gives birth to intuition. Those who are accustomed to listen to this voice out of the Silence, take it more and more as the instigating motive of their actions; and where others, the average men, wander along the intricate paths of reasoning, they go straight their way, guided through the windings of life by intuition, this superior instinct, as by a strong and unfailing hand.

This faculty which is exceptional, almost abnormal now, will certainly be quite common and natural for the new race, the man of tomorrow. But probably the constant exercise of it will be detrimental to the reasoning faculties. As man possesses no more the extreme physical ability of the monkey, so also will the superman lose the extreme mental ability of man,[8] this ability to deceive himself and others.

Thus, man's road to supermanhood will be open when he declares boldly that all he has yet developed, including the intellect of which he is so rightly and yet so vainly proud, is now no longer sufficient for him, and that to uncase, discover, set free this greater power within, shall be henceforward his great preoccupation. Then will his philosophy, art, science, ethics, social existence, vital pursuits be no longer an exercise of mind and life for themselves, in a circle, but a means for the discovery of a greater Truth behind mind and life and the bringing of its power into our human existence. And this discovery is that of our real, because our highest self and nature.

However, that self which we are not yet, but have to become, is not the strong vital Will hymned by Nietzsche, but a spiritual self and spiritual nature. For as soon as we speak of supermanhood we must be careful to avoid all confusion with the strong but so superficial and incomplete conception of Nietzsche's superman.

Indeed, since Nietzsche invented the word superman, when someone uses it to speak of the coming race, willingly or not, it evokes at the same time Nietzsche's conception. Certainly, his idea that to develop the superman out of our present very unsatisfactory manhood is our real business, is in itself an absolutely sound idea; certainly, his formula of our aim, "to become ourselves", implying, as it does, that man has not yet found all his true self, his true nature by which he can successfully and spontaneously live, could not be bettered; nevertheless, Nietzsche made the mistake we said we ought

---

[8] Alternative ending (from earlier draft): perhaps all of the power of reasoning; and even, the organ itself may become useless, disappear little by little as the monkey's tail, which was of no use for man, disappeared from his physical body.

to avoid: his superman is but a man aggrandised, magnified, in whom Force has become super-dominant, crushing under its weight all the other attributes of man. Such cannot be our ideal. We see too well at present whither leads the exclusive worshipping of Force – to the crimes of the strong and the ruin of continents.

No, the way to supermanhood lies in the unfolding of the ever-perfect Spirit. All would change, all would become easy if man could once consent to be spiritualised. The higher perfection of the spiritual life will come by a spontaneous obedience of spiritualised man to the truth of his own realised being, when he has become himself, found his own real nature; but this spontaneity will not be instinctive and subconscient as in the animal, but intuitive and fully, integrally conscient.

Therefore, the individuals who will most help the future of humanity in the new age, will be those who will recognise a spiritual evolution as the destiny and therefore the great need of the human being, an evolution or conversion of the present type of humanity into a spiritualised humanity, even as the animal man has been largely converted into a highly mentalised humanity.

They will be comparatively indifferent to particular belief and form of religion, and leave men to resort to the beliefs and forms to which they are naturally drawn. They will only hold as essential the faith in the spiritual conversion. They will especially not make the mistake of thinking that this change can be effected by machinery and outward institutions; they will know and never forget that it has to be lived out by each man inwardly or it can never be made a reality.

And among these individuals, woman must be the first to realise this great change, as it is her special task to give birth in this world to the first specimens of the new race. And to be able to do this she must, more or less, conceive what will be the practical results of this spiritual conversion. For if it cannot be effected simply by exterior transformations, it can neither be realised without bringing forth such transformations.

These will certainly not be less in the moral and social domains than in the intellectual.

As religious beliefs and cults will become secondary, so also the ethical restrictions or prescriptions, rules of conduct or conventions will lose their importance.[9]

Actually, in human life, the whole moral problem is concentrated in the conflict between the vital will with its impulses and the mental power with its decrees. When the vital will is submitted to the mental power, then the life of the individual or of the society becomes moral. But it is only when both, vital will and mental power, are equally submissive to something higher, to the supermind, that human life is exceeded, that true spiritual life begins, the life of the superman; for his law will come from within, it will be the divine law shining in the centre of each being and governing life from therein, the divine law multiple in its manifestation but one in its origin. And because of its unity this law is the law of supreme order and harmony.

Thus the individual, no more guided by egoistical motives, laws or customs, shall abandon all selfish aims. His rule will

---

9 *This paragraph and the two which precede it replace the following passage of an earlier draft:*

But among these individuals woman, as we have already said, will have one special task to accomplish, that of giving birth in this world to the first specimens of the new race. And to be able to do this we must, more or less, conceive first in our thoughts the ideal of what the superman can be.

Of course, nothing is more difficult than to draw a picture of what will be the new race; it is an almost unrealizable attempt, and we shall certainly not try to enter into details; for we cannot ask of our mind to grasp with any certainty or accuracy this creation of the supermind, of the spirit.

But as we have already seen that the replacing of mental reason by intuitive knowledge will be one of the characteristic features of the future being, in the same way, morally and socially what can be the standard of the new race's life?

From the ethical point of view, for the individual of the new race there will certainly be no more restrictions or prescriptions, rules of conduct or conventions.

be perfect disinterestedness. To act in view of a personal profit, either in this world or in another beyond, will become an unthinkable impossibility. For each act will be done in complete, simple, joyful obedience to the divine law which inspires it, without any seeking for reward or results, as the supreme reward will be in the very delight of acting under such inspiration, of being identified in conscience and will with the divine principle within oneself.

And in this identification the superman will find also his social standard. For in discovering the divine law in himself he will recognise the same divine law in every being, and by being identified with it in himself he will be identified with it in all, thus becoming aware of the unity of all, not only in essence and substance but also in the most exterior planes of life and form. He will not be a mind, a life or a body, but the informing and sustaining Soul or Self, silent, peaceful, eternal, that possesses them; and this Soul or Self he will find everywhere sustaining and informing and possessing all lives and minds and bodies. He will be conscious of this Self as the divine creator and doer of all works, one in all existences; for the many souls of the universal manifestation are only faces of the one Divine. He will perceive each being to be the universal Divinity presenting to him many faces; he will merge himself in That and perceive his own mind, life and body as only one presentation of the Self, and all whom we, at present, conceive of as others will be to his consciousness his own self in other minds, lives and bodies. He will be able to feel his body one with all bodies, as he will be aware constantly of the unity of all matter; he will unite himself in mind and heart with all existences; in short, he will see and feel his own person in all others and all others in himself, realising thus true solidarity in the perfection of unity.

But we must limit to these indispensable hints our description of the superman, and push no further our attempt to picture him, as we are convinced that any endeavour to be more precise would prove not only vain but useless. For it is not a number of imaginings, more or less exact, which can help us in the formation of the future type. It is by holding firm in our heart and mind the dynamism, the irresistible impetus given by a sincere and ardent aspiration, by maintaining in ourselves a certain state of enlightened receptivity towards the supreme Idea of the new race which wills to be manifested on earth, that we can take a decisive step in the formation of the sons of the future, and make ourselves fit to serve as intermediaries for the creation of those who shall save Humanity.[10]

---

[10] *Alternate ending (from an earlier draft)*: of the saviours of the world.
The earlier draft closes with the following additional paragraph:
For, in truth, saviours they will be, as each being of this new type will not live either for himself or for State or society, for the individual ego or the collective ego, but for something much greater, for God in himself and for god in the world.

PRAYERS AND MEDITATIONS
DECEMBER 5TH, 1916

Thou hast granted me the grace of Thy repose in which all individual limits are dissolved, in which one is in all and, more clearly still, all is in oneself. But the mind, merged in this divine ecstasy, cannot yet find any power of expression.

(Factual notation of the experience)

"Turn towards the earth." The usual injunction was heard in the silence of the immutable identification. Then the consciousness became that of the One in all. "Everywhere and in all those in whom thou canst see the One, there will awake the consciousness of this identity with the Divine. Look, it was a Japanese street brilliantly illuminated by gay lanterns picturesquely adorned with vivid colours. And as gradually what was conscious moved on down the street, the Divine appeared, visible in everyone and everything. One of the lightly-built houses became transparent, revealing a woman seated on a tatami in a sumptuous violet kimono embroidered with gold and bright colours. The woman was beautiful and must have been between thirty-five and forty. She was playing a golden samisen. At her feet lay a little child. And in the woman too the Divine was visible.

Prayers and Meditations
December 20th, 1916

The days have gone by, stormy and troubled to all appearance but calm and strong in their reality reflecting Thy divine will; they have gone by, deploying, disclosing, developing once more all the unexpected and varied splendour of Thy untiring divine play. And how marvellous it is to watch this when one perceives the infinite crisscrossing of the movements Thy eternal will creates, when one knows that all this is from all eternity and that it is only in our imperfect faculties that it becomes an uninterrupted succession of facts, in which we are gratuitous and ignorant actors. We act with the apparent unconsciousness and blindness of those who do not know, and yet, I do know and, even while being an actor, I am a spectator too. But I am still not pure enough for Thee to unveil before my eyes the totality of the effects and results; it is only partially and imperfectly that I know them before the act and am permitted to act with the knowledge of the "why", with a full illumination as to what Thou expectest from me. When, 0 Lord, shall I have this purity? But for that too I am no longer impatient and no longer implore. I see how much Thy splendours are obscured and veiled in this miserable and poor instrument; but Thou, Thou knowest why it is thus; and these its shadows and weaknesses Thou dost also use for Thy eternal ends.

My soul is in prayer and bows down in love before what it can understand and know of Thee. My soul is in prayer and gives itself unreservedly to Thee in one of those sublime fervours

which culminate in identification. My soul is in prayer.., and my body too; and my thought is silent in a mute ecstasy.

(Communication received at 5.30 in the evening after meditation.)

"As thou art contemplating me, I shall speak to thee this evening. I see in thy heart a diamond surrounded by a golden light. It is at once pure and warm, something which may manifest impersonal love; but why dost thou keep this treasure enclosed in that dark casket lined with deep purple? The outermost covering is of a deep lustreless blue, a real mantle of darkness. It would seem that thou art afraid of showing thy splendour. Learn to radiate and do not fear the storm: the wind carries us far from the shore but shows us over the world. Wouldst thou be thrifty of thy tenderness? But the source of love is infinite. Dost thou fear to be misunderstood? But where hast thou seen man capable of understanding the Divine? And if the eternal truth finds in thee a means of manifesting itself, what dost thou care for all the rest? Thou art like a pilgrim coming out of the sanctuary; standing on the threshold in front of the crowd, he hesitates before revealing his precious secret, that of his supreme discovery. Listen, I too hesitated for days, for I could foresee both my preaching and its results: the imperfection of expression and the still greater imperfection of understanding. And yet I turned to the earth and men and brought them my message. Turn to the earth and men – this the command thou always hearest in thy heart? — in thy heart, for it is that which carries a blessed message for those who are athirst for compassion. Henceforth nothing can attack the diamond. It is unassailable in its perfect constitution and the soft radiance that flashes from it can change many things in the hearts of men. Thou doubtest thy power and fearest thy ignorance? It is precisely this that wraps up thy strength in that dark mantle of starless night. Thou hesitatest and tremblest as on the threshold of a mystery, for now the mystery of the manifestation seems to thee more terrible and unfathomable than that of the Eternal Cause. But thou must take courage again and obey the injunction from the depths. It is I who am telling thee this, for I know thee and love thee as thou didst know and love me once. I have appeared clearly before thy sight so that thou mayst in no way doubt my word. And also to thy eyes I have shown thy heart so that thou canst thus see what the supreme Truth has willed for it, so that thou mayst discover in it the law of thy being. The thing still seems to thee quite difficult: a day will come when thou wilt wonder how for so long it could have been otherwise"...

Säkyamuni

Prayers and Meditations
January 29ᵗʰ, 1917

In the world of forms a violation of Beauty is as great a fault as a violation of Truth in the world of ideas. For Beauty is the worship Nature offers to the supreme Master of the universe; Beauty is the divine language in forms. And a consciousness of the Divine which is not translated externally by an understanding and expression of Beauty would be an incomplete consciousness.

But true Beauty is as difficult to discover, to understand and above all to live as any other expression of the Divine; this discovery and expression exacts as much impersonality and renunciation of egoism as that of Truth or Bliss. Pure Beauty is universal and one must be universal to see and recognise it.

O Lord of Beauty, how many faults I have committed against Thee, how many do I still commit... Give me the perfect understanding of Thy Law so that I may not again fail to keep it. Love would be incomplete without Thee, Thou art one of its most perfect ornaments, Thou art one of its most harmonious smiles. At times I have misunderstood Thy role, but in the depths of my heart I have always loved Thee; and the most arbitrary and radical doctrines could not extinguish the fire of worship which, from my childhood, I had vowed to Thee.

Thou art not at all what a vain people think Thee to be, Thou art not at all attached exclusively to this or that form of life: it is possible to awaken Thee and make Thee shine in every form; but, for that one must have discovered Thy secret...

O Lord of Beauty, give me the perfect understanding of Thy Law, so that I may no longer fail to keep it, so that Thou mayst become in me the harmonious consummation of the Lord of Love.

Prayers and Meditations
April 1ˢᵗ, 1917

Thou hast shown to my mute and expectant soul all the splendour of fairy landscapes: trees at festival and lonely paths that seem to scale the sky.

But of my destiny Thou didst not speak to me. Must it be so veiled from me?...

Once more, everywhere I see cherry trees; Thou hast put a magical power in the flowers: they seem to speak of Thy sole Presence; they bring with them the smile of the Divine.

My body is at rest and my soul blossoms in light: what kind of a charm hast Thou put into these trees in flower?

O Japan, it is thy festive adorning, expression of thy goodwill, it is thy purest offering, the pledge of thy fidelity; it is thy way of saying that thou dost mirror the sky.

And now here is a magnificent country, of high mountains all covered with pines and richly tilled valleys. And the little pink roses this Chinese brings, are they a promise of the near future?

Prayers and Meditations
April 7ᵗʰ, 1917

A deep concentration seized on me, and I perceived that I was identifying myself with a single cherry-blossom, then through it with all cherry-blossoms, and, as I descended deeper in the consciousness, following a stream of bluish force, I became suddenly the cherry-tree itself, stretching towards the sky like so many arms its innumerable branches laden with their sacrifice of flowers. Then I heard distinctly this sentence:

"Thus hast thou made thyself one with the soul of the cherry-trees and so thou canst take note that it is the Divine who makes the offering of this flower-prayer to heaven."

When I had written it, all was effaced; but now the blood of the cherry-tree flows in my veins and with it flows an incomparable peace and force. What difference is there between the human body and the body of a tree? In truth, there is none: the consciousness which animates them is identically the same.

Then the cherry-tree whispered in my ear:

"It is in the cherry-blossom that lies the remedy for the disorders of the spring."

Goddess Kwannon

THE MOTHER AND THE ARTISTIC SENSIBILITY OF JAPAN

by Debashish Banerji

The Mother's engagement with the artistic sensibility of Japan could be traced back to her decision, as a girl, to train as an artist. In her preteen years, she was taught privately by an art teacher, Marie Bricka, and later, in her teen years, joined a studio of the Academie Julian in Paris. In an essay titled "The Mother as an Artist" we learn that "on the technical side, there was an emphasis on drawing and a resistance to new trends which revelled in pure colour and pattern. The Mother's paintings and drawings certainly attest to her having received the kind of thorough classical training offered by the Academie Julian, though she soon went beyond the formulas of the French 'academic' style." The "new trends which revelled in pure colour and pattern" referred to here were part of the revolution in art inaugurated by the Impressionists that had become normalized in France by the 1890s, when the Mother was in art school, leading to what has been called "Academic Impressionism". It is interesting to note that the premier Japanese artist of the time in the movement known as *yoga* (Western-style painting), Kuroda Sew (1866-1924), trained in such a style in Paris from 1886-93.

The Mother herself refers to her interest in these "new trends" in contrast to the "classical" style when she talks about the milieu of her young days as an artist: "here was an entire very beautiful period (I don't say this because I myself was painting) but all the artists I knew at that time were truly artists, they were serious and did admirable things which have remained admirable. It was the period of the Impressionists; it was the period of Manet, it was a beautiful period, they did beautiful things." She also details the technique of "broken colour" which many of them followed: "The technique is to apply the colours by dots and short lines very close to one another but not to mix; it gives a much more living effect than the mixing and expresses well the play of colours and of light...you can make in that way all possible shades." In the Mother's paintings done in Paris and Algeria, before her visit to Japan, we already see the use of this technique in several paintings.

The revolution in painting inaugurated by the Impressionisits from the third quarter of the nineteenth century owed much to Japan. It is generally supposed that this was due to exposure to woodcut prints (ukiyo-e), but the optical and ontological stagnation represented by "classical" art that these artists sought to overcome was achieved through a variety of new ways of seeing and execution derived from Japan. One may identify three principal features of this adaptation: (1) an emphasis on direct brushed strokes over line drawing; (2) an eye to the placement of objects relative to each other and to the whole, that is, composition and design; and (3) a flattening of perspective. The first of these, the emphasis on direct brushed strokes, is a controversial feature, since it is certainly not found in woodcuts nor in the predominant trend to emphasize outlines. However, it can be thought of as an extension of the calligraphic line, partaking of the same spontaneity in execution, but applied here in terms of colour and texture. This emphasis hearkens back to the first of the six principles of painting canonical to most East Asian painting, as enunciated by Xie He, the Chinese art theoretician of the late fifth century. This is "animation through spirit consonance; a principle that the Mother must have related to the direct animation of the hands by consciousness, something she identified as essential to execution in all the arts. Interestingly, the second principle, "structural method in the use of the brush", in conjunction with the first, is what led to the desirability for spontaneous delineation of outline, analogous in calligraphy and art. But, though the importance of line and its relation with framework, volume and negative space in East Asian art cannot be denied, a tradition of "boneless" painting going back to Mi Fu and others of the Northern Song dynasty and followed by great masters of China and Japan through the centuries, can also be traced. To what extent the Impressionists were conscious of this is difficult to tell. They may have arrived at it independently, but it is unlikely that they saw anything related to consciousness in this, as the Mother seems to have done from the start. Later, she was to find the explicit acknowledgment of this when she went to Japan.

Composition and design correspond to the fifth of Xie He's principles - "dividing and planning, positioning and arranging." In Japanese painting, this element took on a place of prime importance, related to the aesthetics of space. This is certainly something the Impressionists discovered in woodblock prints and used to great effect in their paintings. The making of novelty in composition into a prime aesthetic factor, so as to attract attention and become an integral part of the painting, brought to the fore the mental subjective element, just as spontaneous brushwork could be said to bring forward the vital subjective element. This subjective turn could open the door to something even deeper, a principle of spiritual Beauty, which flooded form and design with its significances. The Mother, who followed her own guidance in developing her artistic sensibility, later expressed the special power of vision of an artist in terms of this kind of proportional and compositional sense:

There is a considerable difference between the vision of ordinary people and the vision of artists. Their way of seeing things is much more complete and conscious than that of ordinary people. When one has not trained one's vision, one sees vaguely, imprecisely, and has impressions rather than an exact vision. An artist, when he sees something and has learned to use his eyes, sees - for instance, when he sees a face, instead of seeing just a form, like that, you know, a form, the general effect of a form...- sees the exact structure of the figure, the proportions of the different parts, whether the figure is harmonious or not, and why;...all sorts of things at one glance, you understand, in a single vision, as one sees the relations between different forms.

This sense of spatial harmony heightened to express spiritual beauty is something that the Mother carried with her to Japan, and discovered there in extraordinary expressions which opened up in her profound spiritual experiences (as we will see).

I have pointed to the flattening of perspective as the third aspect of Japanese painting adapted by Impressionism and internalized by the Mother even prior to her visit to Japan. If spontaneous brushwork and power of composition form vital and mental innovations in Western modernism, this is more essential and may be considered an ontological factor. Yet it isn't made a principle in East Asian art. This is because the sense of completed separation between objects implied in the visuality of the third dimension is not quite as radical in the East Asian (and for that matter, South Asian) experience. The two-dimensionality of Asian painting is not a projection or reduction of a three-dimensional space but a representation of the ground of being, from which beings arise and to which they are anchored. This is also clearly a spiritual principle, a unitary foundation of being, whose mood or quality was conveyed through negative space and colour. European post-Renaissance naturalism, on the other hand, made the representation of three-dimensional reality a principle, accomplished through the devices of perspective, modelling and chiaroscuro (light-and-shade). The exposure to Japanese painting opened the founders of Impressionism to this new intuition of space, but they were left with the problem of moving from a three-dimensional space to this new visuality. They approached this through a variety of means, sometimes through a continuity in gradations of colour and sometimes through the use of thin or flattened perspective. The initiating instance of Impressionism, Monet's Impression, Sunrise, shows the first of these two methods at work. Sea and sky merge into one another, the "depth" of the painting overcome through colour continuity and variation. In the Mother's landscape paintings, we find the use of both the methods mentioned above.

The Mother followed the general artistic interest in Japan (Japonisme) of her times in making a copy of a geisha with a lantern in oils, evidently from a woodcut. Geishas were a principal theme of ukiyo-e prints and when she visited Japan from 1916 to 1920, the Mother collected a few such prints, by reputed artists such as Suzuki Harunobu, the first maker of multicolour prints (nishiki-e) and Kitagawa Utamaro, perhaps the best of the geisha print designers. Other popular Japanese objects of interest in France included lacquer boxes, dolls, fans and notepads, and the Mother collected instances of many of these objects. In her training as an artist, the Mother was led from within by a spiritual intuition. When she went to Japan in 1916, she found explicit affirmation of her intuitions in the pedagogical ideas and cultural expressions of Japan. She also found the extension of the principles of composition, colour, animistic sensibility and sense of space in all aspects of Japanese life of the senses, particularly the visual, making up the fabric of social life. She has spoken on a number of occasions about how "Japan is essentially the country of sensations; she lives through her eyes. Beauty rules over her as an uncontested master." In this she has noted how integrated the sensibility of visual beauty is at all levels of Japanese life - "very simple people, men of the working class or even peasants go for rest or enjoyment to a place where they can see a beautiful landscape" - and how attuned such a life is with nature's temporal moods - "for each season there are known sites. For instance, in autumn leaves become red;

they have large numbers of maple-trees (the leaves of the maple turn into all the shades of the most vivid red in autumn, it is absolutely marvellous), so they arrange a place near a temple, for instance, on the top of a hill, and the entire hill is covered with maples."

The power of such a sensibility to induce spiritual experiences is attested to by her in a number of instances. For example, even when she was a child in France, before knowing anything about Japanese gardens, it is as if her encounter of the future prefigured itself to her in visions where she saw scenes which she took to be of some heavenly world; and which she recognized physically later when she visited Japan.

'The other day I spoke to you about those landscapes of Japan; well, almost all - the most beautiful, the most striking ones - I had seen in vision in France; and yet I had not seen any pictures or photographs of Japan, I knew nothing of Japan. And I had seen these landscapes without human beings, nothing but the landscape, quite pure, like that, and it had seemed to me they were visions of a world other than the physical; they seemed to me too beautiful for the physical world, too perfectly beautiful. Particularly I used to see very often those stairs rising straight up into the sky; in my vision there was the impression of climbing straight up, straight up, and as though one could go on climbing, climbing, climbing... It had struck me, and the first time I saw this in Nature down there, I understood that I had already seen it in France before having known anything about Japan.'

Elsewhere, she has described these stairs passing through a maple garden as she saw them in Japan, where families visit in autumn:

There is a stairway which climbs straight up, almost like a ladder, from the base to the top, and it is so steep that one cannot see what is at the top, one gets the feeling of a ladder rising to the skies - a stone stairway, very well made, rising steeply and seeming to lose itself in the sky - clouds pass, and both the sides of the hill are covered with maples, and these maples have the most magnificent colours you could ever imagine. Well, an artist who goes there will experience an emotion of absolutely exceptional, marvellous beauty. But one sees very small children, families even, with a baby on the shoulder, going there in groups. In autumn they will go there.

Similarly, she refers to the enjoyment of viewing cherry trees in blossom in spring:

Just at the beginning of spring...,there are the first cherry-trees. These cherry-trees never give fruit, they are grown only for the flowers. They range from white to pink, to a rather vivid pink. There are long avenues all bordered with cherry trees, all pink; they are huge trees which have turned all pink. There are entire mountains covered with these cherry-trees, and on the little rivulets bridges have been built which too are all red: you see these bridges of red lacquer among all these pink flowers and, below, a great river flowing and a mountain which seems to scale the sky.

And corresponding to this, we find her description of her experience of identity with the spirit of the cherry trees in her *Prayers and Meditations*:

A deep concentration seized on me, and I perceived that I was identifying myself with a single cherry-blossom, then through it with all cherry-blossoms, and, as I descended deeper in the consciousness, following a stream of bluish force, I became suddenly the cherry-tree itself, stretching towards the sky like so many arms its innumerable branches laden with their sacrifice of flowers. Then I heard distinctly this sentence: "Thus hast thou made thyself one with the soul of the cherry-trees and so thou canst take note that it is the Divine who makes the offering of this flower-prayer to heaven." When I had written it, all was effaced; but now the blood of the cherry-tree flows in my veins and with it flows an incomparable peace and force.

It is interesting to note the animistic content of this experience and relate it to the first of Xie He's principles of painting that we discussed earlier: "animation through spirit consonance." This implies an ability to identify with the vital spirit of things through heightened concentration, allowing oneself to be moved by it, as in calligraphic brushwork.

Perhaps most of all, she was struck by the sensibility of arrangement, of the harmony of parts and whole, which she found everywhere in Japan. When she speaks of this, she expresses it as a general principle which was present in all great pre-modern cultures but is largely lost except in Japan:

True art is a whole and an ensemble; it is one and of one piece with life. You see something of this intimate wholeness in ancient Greece and ancient Egypt; for there pictures and statues and all objects of art were made and arranged as part of the architectural plan of a building, each detail a portion of the whole. It is like that in Japan, or at least it was so till the other day before the invasion of a utilitarian and practical modernism. A Japanese house is a wonderful artistic whole; always the right thing is there in the right place, nothing wrongly set, nothing too much, nothing too little. Everything is just as it needed to be, and the house itself blends marvellously with the surrounding nature.

Corresponding to such a house in its street setting, we find one of her most beautiful experiences:

It was a Japanese street brilliantly illuminated by gay lanterns picturesquely adorned with vivid colours. And as gradually what was conscious moved on down the street, the Divine appeared, visible in everyone and everything. One of the lightly-built houses became transparent, revealing a woman seated on a tatami in a sumptuous violet kimono embroidered with gold and bright colours. The woman was beautiful and must have been between thirty-five and forty. She was playing a golden samisen. At her feet lay a little child. And in the woman too the Divine was visible.

While she was in Japan, the Mother painted a few portraits and some landscapes in oil. In these the principles of spontaneous brushwork, compositional novelty and thin perspective are all at work. She also tried her hand at ink painting and took back with her some ink brushes, an ink-and-brush calligraphic set and an example of spontaneous ink painting (sumi-e). In Pondicherry, she found little time to paint, but made a few oil paintings and a number of portraits with pencil, ink-pen and ink-and-brush. Particularly the ink-and-brush portraits evidence strongly the Japanese conception of calligraphic outline and realism through minimalism. In Pondicherry, the Mother's engagement with the artistic sensibility of Japan continued to express itself, and found perhaps its most integrated expression in the spatial and material principles she could manifest in collaboration with architects Antonin Raymond, François Sammer, and George Nakashima, whom Sri Aurobindo named Sundarananda (Delight-in-Beauty), in the construction and use of the guest house, Golconde. Here the modernist principles of functional built environments as residential space were combined with the visual and tactile elegance of Japanese life and an attention to consciousness in material things, which formed part of Sri Aurobindo and the Mother's Integral Yoga.

- Debashish Banerji

Debashish is the Haridas Chaudhuri Professor of Indian Philosophy and Culture and the Doshi Professor of Asian Art at the California Institute of Integral Studies, San Francisco. He has curated a number of exhibitions of Indian and Japanese art and is the author of two books: The Alternate Nation of

Abanindranath Tagore (Sage, 2010) and Seven Quartets of Becoming: A Transformational Yoga Psychology Based on the Diaries of Sri Aurobindo (DK Printworld and Nalanda International, 2012).

Mme Nobuko Kobayashi met the Mother again when she visited India
and the Sri Aurobindo Ashram in Pondicherry, 1959

Recent photo of the house in which Mother lived near Shichi-jyo street in
Kyoto 1917-1920

84

A woodblock print from Kitagawa Utamaru, 1753-1806 (a reproduction),
was acquired by the Mother in Japan

PHOTO REFERENCES

Cover Page
Roof of the Daiunji Temple in Kyoto, painting by the Mother.
Oil on board. Signed Ma (monogram) 15 x 22.5cm, 1918. Japan.

Page 12
The Richards made friends with Japanese intellectuals and with the
leaders of certain "New Life" Movements.
They also met Rabindranath Tagore, during his tour of Japan,
who was impressed by them both.

Page 15
In Kyoto with Mme Nobuko Kobayashi.

Page 19
Japanese Poet Hirasawa Tetsuo. This excellent portrait of poet and
artist Hirasawa Tetsuo is still in fairly good condition. It was done
in one sitting. Hirasawa later visited the Mother in Pondicherry.
(October 1924). Oil on board. 19 x 14 cm. 1916-20. Japan.

Page 47
In Tokyo, 1916, with Paul Richard, Datta, and Japanese friends.

Page 51
During her stay at Kyoto, the Mother developed
a deep friendship with Mme Kobayashi.

Page 65
Image of The Buddha. This small painting was probably started by
a student and finished by the Mother.
Oil on board. 14 x 8.5cm. 1920-30. Pondicherry.

Page 72
Image of Goddess Kwannon, A painting of the Japanese goddess
Jwannon, Goddess of Mercy. It was done for the cover of a book in
Bengali by Nolini Kanta Gupta, Narir Katha. C. 1930. Pondicherry.

Text References

The Mother, The story of Her Life, Georges Van Vrekhem
Harper Collins Publishers, India, 2000

Words of Long Ago, CWM, Vol. 2
Sri Aurobindo Trust, 1980

Words of The Mother, CWM, Vol. 14
Sri Aurobindo Trust, 1980

Mother's Agenda, August 8, 1964, pp. 150-151

Questions and Answers 1950-51, CWM, Vol. 4
Sri Aurobindo Trust, 1972

Questions and Answers 1953, CWM, Vol. 5
Sri Aurobindo Trust, 1976

Prayers and Meditations, CWM, Vol. 1
Sri Aurobindo Trust, 1980

Other books published by PRISMA

Antithesis of Yoga
by Jocelyn

Finding the Psychic Being
by Loretta Shartsis

The Mother on Japan
by The Mother

The Teachings of Flowers
(The Life and Work of the Mother of the
Sri Aurobindo Ashram)
by Loretta Shartsis

Death doesn't exist
The Mother on Death, Sri Aurobindo on Rebirth
by The Mother

Passage to More than India
by Dick Batstone

The Supramental Transformation
by Loretta Shartsis

Children of Change: A Spiritual Pilgrimage
by Amrit

Memories of Auroville - told by early Aurovilians
by Janet Fearn

Bougainvilleas PROTECTION
by Narad (Richard Eggenberger), Nilisha Mehta

The Mother's Yoga - 1956-1973 (Vol. 1, 1956-1967)
by Loretta Shartsis

The Mother's Yoga - 1956-1973 (Vol. 2, 1968-1973)
by Loretta Shartsis

Crossroad The New Humanity
by Paulette Hadnagy

www.ingramcontent.com/pod-product-compliance
Lightning Source LLC
LaVergne TN
LVHW011047200726
843509LV00011B/1360

9 789395 460064